First Field Trips

Public Library

by Cari Meister

Bullfrog Books

Ideas for Parents and Teachers

Bullfrog Books let children practice reading informational text at the earliest reading levels. Repetition, familiar words, and photo labels support early readers.

Before Reading

- Discuss the cover photo. What does it tell them?

- Look at the picture glossary together. Read and discuss the words.

Read the Book

- "Walk" through the book and look at the photos. Let the child ask questions. Point out the photo labels.

- Read the book to the child, or have him or her read independently.

After Reading

- Prompt the child to think more. Ask: Have you ever visited your public library? Did you check out any books? What is your favorite kind of book to read?

Bullfrog Books are published by Jump!
5357 Penn Avenue South
Minneapolis, MN 55419
www.jumplibrary.com

Library of Congress Cataloging-in-Publication Data

Names: Meister, Cari, author.
Title: Public library / by Cari Meister.
Description: Minneapolis, MN : Jump!, Inc. [2016] |
Series: First field trips | Includes index.
Identifiers: LCCN 2015032573 |
ISBN 9781620312964 (hardcover: alk. paper) |
ISBN 9781624963629 (ebook)
Subjects: LCSH: Libraries—Juvenile literature. |
Public libraries—Juvenile literature. |
School field trips—Juvenile literature.
Classification: LCC Z665.5.M45 2016 |
DDC 027.4—dc23
LC record available at http://lccn.loc.gov/2015032573

Editor: Jenny Fretland VanVoorst
Series Designer: Ellen Huber
Book Designer: Lindaanne Donohoe
Photo Researcher: Lindaanne Donohoe

Photo Credits: All photos by Shutterstock except: 123RF, 16–17; Corbis, 14, 18–19; Dreamstime, 10, 11; Getty, 23tr; iStock, 1, 5, 6–7, 15; Popartic/Shutterstock.com, 23br; Thinkstock, 4, 12–13, 22.

Printed in the United States of America at Corporate Graphics in North Mankato, Minnesota.

Table of Contents

Book Fun 4

At the Library 22

Picture Glossary 23

Index 24

To Learn More 24

Book Fun

Where is the class going?

To the library!

Bo is a librarian.

She helps people.

She finds books.

She finds information.

Ssh!

It is story time.

Bo reads.

It is a funny book.

This is the catalog.
It shows what the library has.

It has books.

It has DVDs.

It has magazines.

Li wants a book about cats.

She types CAT in the search bar.

Wow!

There are 20 books!

TJ finds a book about cars.

Peg finds a DVD.

Our teacher found
a book, too!

He scans his library card.

He scans his book.

When are the
books due?

In two weeks.

The library was fun.
Let's go back soon.

At the Library

shelves
Books are organized on shelves so that people can find them easily.

computer
Libraries have computers that people can use for research.

desk
Libraries have desks where people can work.

reading area
Libraries have comfortable seating areas for people to read.

Picture Glossary

DVD
A plastic disk on which information, such as computer data or a movie, is stored.

library card
A card that gives holders permission to borrow library materials.

librarian
A person in charge of a library.

magazine
A publication containing multiple articles and issued at regular intervals.

Index

books 6, 9, 11, 12, 14, 17, 18

catalog 10

class 4

due 18

DVDs 11, 15

information 6

librarian 6

library card 17

magazines 11

reading 9

story time 9

To Learn More

Learning more is as easy as 1, 2, 3.

1) Go to www.factsurfer.com

2) Enter "publiclibrary" into the search box.

3) Click the "Surf" button to see a list of websites.

With factsurfer.com, finding more information is just a click away.

24